# In the Care of Plenty

# *In the Care of Plenty*

## Poems

Allan Hugh Cole Jr.

RESOURCE *Publications* • Eugene, Oregon

IN THE CARE OF PLENTY
Poems

Resource Publications
An Imprint of Wipf and Stock Publishers
199 W. 8th Ave., Suite 3
Eugene, OR 97401

www.wipfandstock.com

PAPERBACK ISBN: 978-1-6667-0274-3
HARDCOVER ISBN: 978-1-6667-0275-0
EBOOK ISBN: 978-1-6667-0276-7

.                                                    OCTOBER 5, 2021 1:27 PM

For Michael Adams and Elizabeth Gaucher

But I have promises to keep,

And miles to go before I sleep.

ROBERT FROST

# Contents

### III

# Acknowledgments

I AM GRATEFUL FOR several people who inspired the poems in this book or helped improve them. A particular word of thanks goes to those at Wipf and Stock Publishers, especially Matthew Wimer, Editorial Production Manager, for his keen editorial guidance. I have been fortunate to work with Wipf and Stock on several books and doing so continues to be a pleasure.

Laura Dosanjh, a wise therapist and doctoral student in the Steve Hicks School of Social Work at The University of Texas at Austin (UT), where I work as a professor and administrator, read all of these poems and shared her typically perceptive and helpful insights. Mia Vinton, my colleague in the Steve Hicks School, assisted with editorial matters along with helping me find time in a typically full schedule to write. I am grateful for Laura and Mia's generosity and support.

An unanticipated gift of having young-onset Parkinson's disease has been meeting smart, kind, generous, funny, and devoted people who also live with this illness. One of these people, Michael Adams, came into my life just as I began to write this book. Michael has served for more than 15 years as the director of the Dobie Paisano Fellowship Program for writers at UT. His wisdom and experience tied to a career of teaching others to write better, not to mention his talents as a novelist and painter, converged with his abiding generosity to help me write better poems and, on my best days, to think of myself as an improving poet. I am in his debt for all of this, but mostly I am grateful for his friendship and kindness toward me. Of course, Michael bears no responsibility for anything lacking in these poems!

My longtime friend and writing partner Elizabeth Gaucher, principal at Longridge Editors, has her fingerprints on many things I write, including the poems in this book. As one who lives with a chronic illness herself, she is a kindred spirit who helps me probe deeply into my emotional life to write more authentically and with greater humanity. I remain grateful for her talents, generosity, humor, honesty, and fierce dedication to her craft, all of which inspire and enrich my writing and my life.

Ethan Henderson and Chris Lion, Renaissance men, valued friends and writing companions, and two of my fellow travelers on the Parkinson's road, read all of the poems here and provided helpful feedback that improved them. My friends Jordan Steiker and Lori Holleran Steiker support and encourage me often in my journey with Parkinson's and are also a significant part of this book and a treasured part of my life. Gary Freeman, professor of government emeritus at UT and a dear friend who has Parkinson's, offered thoughtful and wise feedback, as did his partner Joan Yamini, a poet and therapist par excellence. Gary and I meet regularly, often on his front porch, and share our stories and bare our souls. I am grateful for his presence in my life.

The late Donald Capps, a longtime professor at Princeton Seminary and my doctoral advisor and mentor, loved poetry and reflecting on its power, for readers and writers. He taught me many things for which I remain grateful, including how to think in less conventional ways about poetry and writing. I wish he could read this book and that we could talk about it, just as we discussed others' poetry so many times.

My mother, Jeri Cole, and I read and wrote poetry together when I was a child, and I credit her with helping me discover a love for words and books. She and my father, Allan Cole, have never wavered in their support and encouragement, whether relating to Parkinson's or any other facet of my life.

Finally, my wife Tracey and our daughters, Meredith and Holly, who I adore and with whom I am fortunate to share an

## Acknowledgments

abundant life, inspire me to speak more truthfully and coura-
geously and to live with greater authenticity and hope. When not in
the foreground of these poems, they are surely in the background.
With them, I live in the care of plenty.

*I*

## The River

Fresh sunlight
Touches the shallow river,
Its waters flowing toward
Places not yet known.

A warm June breeze blows,
Waking brushy hilltops
Dry from hot
Spring days and nights.

A mourning dove
Sits on a rock and coos,
Calling out to the waters
Snaking through tall banks.

Life unfolds as the river flows,
With waters tranquil and troubled.
What lies around the bend
We do not know.

# Unforeseen

I lie in the imaging room.
A machine hisses and whines.
Radioactive isotopes light up my brain.
My mind flips through a life deemed over.

For almost a year I keep silent.
I hide from others and myself.
I labor through each day.
My secret stays guarded.

I grow tired of hiding.
I feel like a fraud.
I finally share the news.
My children are the catalyst.

I hope I can show them resilience.
Finding meaning and purpose is also my goal.
Illness provides an odd sort of renewal.
I could not be more surprised.

My life is not over.
It is being reshaped and repurposed.
I am discovering new goals and roles.
I am silent no more.

# PERSISTENCE

*(for Meredith)*

Tip of the tongue out, past your lips,
Lithe hands stretching across ivory keys,
Sheet music placed front and center,
Pencil-marked study, notes to remember,

Melodic sounds reflecting hours of work,
Pressing keys with persistent poise,
Smiles alternating with furrowed brows,
Practicing each day, big dreams intact—

Sitting at your piano, you push on,
Just as you do at school and elsewhere.
Your father feels great pride in you,
Celebrates your imagination and creativity,

Admires your wisdom and sense of humor,
Your insights and unconventional ways of seeing,
Your tireless pursuit of learning,
Your big and active brain.

Daily, I observe you,
Learn from you.
I am inspired by your fierce commitment to
What you love—your persistence.

Keep it up, my love.
I'm taking notes of my own.

# DETERMINATION

*(for Holly)*

Big dimples, unleashed by your smile,
Pop with joy and mischief,
Satisfaction, too,

When you figure things out,
Which you so naturally do,
Working a problem and staying the course.

Your kindness and compassion are also big.
Intelligent and curious,
Your zest for life shows through.

I believe in you.
Believe in yourself, dear one,
Continue to live as you do.

Stand strong in your values and passions,
Stay the course with living true,
Surf your wake, dance your song,

Write your story as you choose,
Knowing that I believe in you,
My dimples popping, too.

# NIGHT

The clock sits on the chest of drawers,
White numbers glowing in the dark.
In the quietest hours, I wonder,
*How will this night unfold?*

Answers come with letting go,
Yielding control, inviting
The sphere of mystery,
Permitting the unknown take hold.

Time crawls toward morning while
My eyes stay open, my brain trying to slow.
I consider the fragileness in every life,
Each filled with joy and pain.

Any moment may change us.
Life-altering experiences abound.
It takes a miracle to get through the day.
And the night.

# WHAT?

Diving deep into
Books and papers,
Hearing lectures whenever I could,
The question that drove me was *Why?*

*Why do we exist?*
*Why do people think and act as they do?*
*Why so much injustice in the world?*
*Why do children suffer?*

*Why* framed my
Existential quests,
Scholarly and personal agendas,
My life's work.

When the shaking palsy shook my life,
Agendas changed, as did my quests and work.
The question of *Why?*
Never crossed my mind.

Instead, I asked, *What?*
*What can I do to live well?*
*What meaning can I discover?*
*What may I do to use Parkinson's for good?*

# HOPE

Healing begins with hope.
No, with a persistent,
Stubborn commitment to
Staying hopeful.

So I pledge hopefulness
Each morning,
Saying to myself,
Sometimes aloud,

*I am grateful for another day.*
*I will do my best to make it good.*
*I will focus on my strengths.*
*I will be hopeful.*

My choice to begin each day
In this way follows
From a belief that hope
Helps us savor the moment,

To recognize that
Today is all we have.
I hold fast to other
Sources of hope:

Family and friends,
What I have, not what I lack,
What I can still do,
Despite Parkinson's

And because of it.
Making meaning with illness,
Confident that my experience matters
Regardless of how it turns out,

Irrespective of finding a cure,
Helps me locate joy in the present.

And to heal.

## Not Yet Complete

I lost my sense of smell.
Now, it requires a hard sniff
To take in lavender shampoo,
Mountain laurel, and
Cookie smells on my daughters' faces.

I lost the ability to sleep.
Medicines that help me move all-day
Prop open my eyes at night,
Brain churning,
Inching toward morning.

I lost my status as illness-free.
Status never meant that
Much to me
Until it rushed off
Without even a hinted warning.

Acceptance of what I lost
Brought inner peace.
Empowerment followed,
Commitments to generosity, too,
Renewing compassion for others and myself.

Each new day
Amid losses and gains,
Surprises and sure things,
I become more me.
A life not yet complete.

# Sanctuary

One of my early memories
Is of a sanctuary,
On a Sunday morning,
Me standing four years tall

Before a silver font,
Water poured over
My wavy brown hair.
Brassy smells, wetness, and

Organ fugues converge
As I see my eyes in the
Silver bowl,
The moment, I am told,

A new life begins,
One offering
Joy and purpose,
The forgiveness of sins.

Nearly fifty years hence,
I sit on the back pew,
Watching similar acts,
Pondering what I know,

Wondering what others
See in the font,
How their lives will go,
What they will lose,

The pews they will choose.
Perhaps they will stand

Near other waters,
Amid different sacred smells,
Textures, and converging sounds,

Where new life
Also begins,
Eyes focus, and
Faith expands.

# Disparity

As heavy traffic drones above their heads,
A winter's sun begins to set,
Returning them to a nightly dread.

A dirty tent under an interstate bridge
Protects them some from wind and rain,
But not from the cold, nor fear, nor pain.

We speak of their child's pending birth.
A bent smile marks her father's face.
We offer them food. I hope for grace.

Whispering to myself, "I have only Parkinson's to manage,"
I wonder if they will find a new place to sleep,
Or have to settle for a bigger tent.

# Church Bells

When church bells ring,
I close my eyes and remember
The grand tracker organ playing hymns
Across a deep, lush gorge,

Just a few feet from
The stately red-brick sanctuary
Over a century old.
Wood stoves puffed oaky smells

Into cloudy cool air as
Mountains on the horizon
Received my prayers.

Was anyone there?

*II*

# STAYING AFLOAT

*(for Tracey)*

Those first months I felt like a man
Treading water in the Atlantic,
Waiting for someone to throw me

A life preserver and pull me to shore.
My cries for help were faint,
Drowned out by internal

Screams before an audience of one.
You floated beside me and let me
Hold on to you, drifting with currents,

Rolling over waves, and ducking under
Whitecaps whose frothy residue
Made it difficult to see and

Sometimes to breathe.
Another was there in those waters
Floating with us,

Keeping us buoyant enough
To hold on to one another and
Stay alive, one wave at a time.

## SCRAPING THE KNEE

Behind me lie paths too lightly worn,
Uncharted ways,
Terrain swiftly spared,
For fear of stumbling and scraping the knee.

At forty-eight,
Playing it safe,
Parkinson's pointed toward
New paths that beckoned:

Do not tread gently,
Run hard and be.
Toss-off caution, delays,
You can still break free.

Still scrape the knee.

# The Front Porch

*(for Gary Freeman)*

Joined by neurologic woes and
Mutual devotion to scholarly pursuits,
We meet on his front porch to remember
Lives before brain protein clumps arrived,
When we woke, spoke, and moved smooth.

Still, remembering is not all we do.

We lament and debate,
Laugh and act young,
Make sense and create,
Speak more freely,
Bare souls and live true.

The memories, brand-new.

# Values

Material excess
Smothers time,
Snatches meaning,
Splits the soul.

Unchecked consumption
Diminishes freedom,
Drains energy,
Detracts from dreamtime.

More seeks for more.
Seconds tick away.

# The Secret

Nearly a year passed
Before I shared
What made my arm stiff,
My sneaker tread wear

Uneven on the left,
My foot sometimes dragging—
Why once while running
I stumbled and fell.

In silence, I feared
What I may lose—
Identity, income,
Status, and dreams.

Anxious over how
I would be seen—
Disabled, less capable—
I withdrew.

With Parkinson's came
Unfamiliar pain,
Loneliness, fear,
Regrets unforeseen,

Made more grueling,
Sorrowful,
By the secret
I would choose.

# My Physician Friend

*(for Roozbeh Taeed)*

My physician friend
Cares for children's hearts,
Logging long days
And longer nights

In a place where
Any parent fears
Should sleep the ones
They cherish most.

A physician by vocation,
By disposition, a man of peace,
His gentle way
Boosts my spirit,

His effortless way of
Goodness and compassion,
Offers calm, sows hope,
Grows my heart's space.

Seeing in him
What I know to be true
Renews my efforts for
Goodness and compassion,

Prompts prayers for his children,
Their parents, too,
Keeping me mindful of
All hearts that ache.

# For One Who Has Lost

When you live the absence of your beloved—
A closed heart, listless soul, lungs gasping for air,

Unending reminders of life disappeared,
Taken so quickly it feels unfair,

Reasons unclear
Days harder to bear—

Beware of bitter despair,
Weighty regrets, unending tears,

Sit each day with memories you shared,
Amid your burdens, let go of fear,

Open your heart,
Your loved one remains near.

# The Teacher

Ardently teaching for twenty years
Fluent in words of resilience and hope
I said to students: "Listen and learn!"

At mid-career, illness began
Invading vessels from
Brain to big toes,

Slowing while showing,
Robbing and rewarding,
Exhausting but enlivening

Confusing and clarifying.
As a Parkinson's student
I listen and learn,

Professing,
Progressing,
Teaching anew.

# Doctors' Words

Future paths open with doctors' words.
Confident or hedging,
Direct or veiled,
Lives are changed with the words they choose.

"I don't make predictions," a doctor once said, and
Not knowing is OK if that's the best one can do.
But an educated guess is not a prediction,
Nor is offering reasons for hope undue.

A best-guess shared with an encouraging tone
May calm a mind untethered, adrift,
Awash in uncertainty about a life with illness,
Feeling afraid and worried— all alone.

A doctor's words may build or destroy,
Predicting how one goes forth
Into one's only life,
Until no path opens.

# Listening

When losing my way—
Disoriented,
Exhausted,
Afraid, and
Despairing—
I listen.

I listen for
Guidance,
Wisdom,
Encouragement,
Significance,
Reasons to persist.

Listening is the point.

When I remain quiet,
My heart opens.
My mind expands.
My spirit expects and
Trusts again,
Full of gratitude and at peace.

Comforted,
Hopeful,
Alive, and
Well,
I find my way once more.

Listening, my compass.

# For the Newly Diagnosed

When you wobble with fear,
Have face-shining tears,
Long for someone to make stable your soul—

When your heart has a hole and the singular goal
Is to stop the bleeding
Lest grief takes its toll—

Hands you may fold, then bend at the knee,
Confront the abyss,
Fearing not what you see—

For despite what wounds your heart or your soul,
You will not be alone,
Nor ever let go.

## The Fall and The Swallow

"Who will go first?"
Says the fall to the swallow,
Two that compete
For a Parkie's demise.

"Go right ahead,"
Says the swallow to the fall,
"I can easily call when
One struggles to rise,

Deciding then whether
One lives or dies."

# MEDICINE

Medicine enters the body's flow,
Resides for a while,
Says "YES" or "NO"
To whether one thrives or labors,
Stays or goes
On to dwell in other, unknown domains,
With no need for medicine
To cover the pain.

# Give and Take

Quelling movement and comfort,
Dignity and grace,

Inflicting stiffness and slowness,
Clumsiness and pain,

Throwing hurdles in front
Of presumed life-paths,

You take relentlessly,
Every day is the same.

And . . .

Inviting openness and courage,
Freedom unknown,

Placing generous ones
On the illness road

Who, unflinchingly brave,
Encourage and companion,

Daring disease to think it will win—
Surprisingly, you give much, too.

# Illness Calls

Illness calls when you least expect it—
Jarring assumptions,
Clouding plans,
Forcing vulnerability previously unknown.

Illness calls for priorities to reset—
For living, working,
Learning, relating,
For deciding what is timeless and true.

Illness calls for habits to change—
More trust and less control,
Living in the present,
Relishing each moment.

Illness calls for compassion to spread—
Toward others and ourselves,
For who we have been,
For who we will become.

# OUR PEOPLE

Our people did not go to college.
Steady work in textile mills was each
Generation's apparent path,
Drawn toward familiar ways,

Honest pay, and a
Lack of pretense.
At my private college,
I had to ask a roommate

What a debutante was,
And "What in the world is
A youth hostel in Europe?"
Our people liked to debut a good story,

Make something with their hands,
Sit at home, plates in laps,
For a long Sunday meal
Where I can still hear

My grandfather's
Cherished harmonica,
Its polished steel making
Twangy country sounds

Rolling over grandchildren
Circled under a thick oak tree.
Laughter interrupted our breathing
As we took turns trying to play it.

For a time, I took these
Sounds for granted,
Told myself that
Life offered better music.

I look at our people differently now,
Seeing those content
To stick with what matters,
To what stays true.

# ONE CLICK

It took a day to write the news,
Nearly an hour to click "Send."
A tremoring index finger touching
Black keys and a smooth mousepad,

Moving me closer to unimagined risk.
Nearly a dozen books written,
Hundreds of students taught,
Fearing decades of work made obsolete.

With one click, a new life begins.

# ARE YOU ANGRY?

People ask if I am angry.
Angry that Parkinson's called at 48.
*No,* I tell them.
*Sad, but not angry.*

Honest.
Anger links to feeling
Wronged or violated,
Mistreated or harmed; or

When any of these
Affect ones we hold dear.
I experienced none of this.
Just the opposite has been true.

Before Parkinson's and since,
I have known good fortune,
Even abundance—
Supportive parents,

A loving partner,
Kind children,
Compassionate friends,
Generous colleagues.

I get to make a living as I teach,
Learn, grow, and serve
Alongside extraordinary people.
Every day.

I would gladly do this work
For free if there were other means
By which to live and
Provide for my family.

I know hundreds of inspiring,
Decent, compassionate,
And dedicated people
Living with Parkinson's, too,

As well as those who support
And care for them.
There's more.
I now experience

A richness of humanity
And joy for living I never
Knew was possible
Before Parkinson's called.

Swimming in good fortune,
In daily abundance,
Living with a new purpose,
How could I feel angry?

# My Kindred

Wide shelves of books reveal
Copious questions,
Quests for understanding,
Longings for purpose.

Philosophy and religion,
Therapies and poetry,
Prized sources of clarity,
Means for gleaning wisdom.

The book has long been
My sacred object,
A go-to companion
In the liminal spaces.

But I need additional companions now.
Always did.
More than intellectual curiosity
I need heartbeats and bodies.

I learned this in midlife
Through illness unexpected,
When I found my kindred
In groups large and small,

In quivering bodies and tenacious spirits,
In those who wake with courage,
Fiery constitutions,
Hearts beating fast,

In people fighting and loving,
Breathing and making a difference,
While knowing they are more than
What ails them.

Vulnerable souls
Exposed in hope
Sustain me now and
Answer more of my questions.

Not every question is answerable
Or will be.
Still, I will keep reading, and
Seeking wisdom with my kin.

# THE LAKE

I think of my illness.
The sun appears.
It makes the water glisten.
Tiny ripples slosh against the boat.

I untie the dock lines.
The tip of one falls into the water.
A catfish rolls out of the way.
I turn the key.

The boat's cold motor chugs.
A thick-bodied drake swims by.
He dips his head and bill.
My eyes follow his path.

# More Than Before

Is the uneasiness yours or mine?
You not knowing what to say,
I fearing you will treat
Me differently in time?

Maybe you wonder if I am the same person,
Or if I will continue to be.
When illness came, I wondered, too,
Questioning if I could still be me.

Turns out I am not the same as before.
To my surprise,
I am different.
I am more.

More attuned to the world,
To others' pain,
To injustice I witness,
To what happens in vain.

More accepting and vulnerable,
Human and brave,
Grateful for what I have,
Expectant of each day.

I also know myself more fully.
You can know me better, too,
For more of me stays present now,
More of me remains accessible to you.

We need not feel uneasy, then,
Only connected, alive, and free,
Grateful we have one another,
More than before.

## Faces

Joy after mastering the Beethoven sonata,
Freedom while painting the fresh winter scene,

A furrowed brow linked to teenaged boys,
Streaming tears when excluded by friends,

Frustration with the geometry proof,
Smiles after getting braces removed,

Anticipation over college choices,
Sleepy eyes after late-night homework.

Dimples showing at the dance recital,
Eyes sparkling after making the team.

I look into their faces,
Seeing reasons to persevere.

# A Long Haul

You think life may end tomorrow
Before learning the disease's course is slow.

"You are looking at thirty to forty years,
Maybe longer," said my doctor,

In younger people, usually,
"This is how Parkinson's goes."

Now, I live for today but
Prepare for the long haul,

For the decades of life with
My constant companion.

I expect to haul tremors and stiffness,
Slowness and cramping,

Sleeplessness and a faulty gait.
Future loads may include

Anxiety and depression,
Constipation and slurred speech,

Losing focus or an ability to multitask.
It's a long haul.

More than our preparations, our companions—
Partners, family,

Friends, and other haulers—
Can give it meaning.

Make it beautiful.
Doctors should say this, too.

# COMFORT

When illness begins,
Hearts ache and
Souls grow heavy.

With time, the infirm learn
A heart is resilient and
Souls can shed weight.

Comfort is the way.
Those we love may comfort us,
We may comfort them.

# Healing

Happiness does not require a cure.
Neither does feeling at peace with illness.
Otherwise, I am sentenced to discontentment,
Gripped by anxiety or resentment.

If happiness presumes wellness
I forego each day's openings—for
Passion and learning, significance and purpose,
For indescribable joy with those I love.

Looking at the horizon for a cure
Must not take my eyes away
From beautiful vistas and
Sacredness before me.

Illness teaches this.
I am also learning that,
While it may surprise us,
Healing can precede cures.

# SOJOURNING

To live is to incur losses—
Our sources of security and pleasure,
Values and purpose,
Even our self-understanding.

This is how we mourn—
We create spaces to hold what we lose,
Where we keep memories and gratitude,
Learnings and hopes, each uniquely ours.

There, we sojourn with them,
Experiencing their presence
When we have the need,
Returning as we desire.

This is how we heal—
Sojourning with our losses,
Forming and nurturing new relationships,
Investing in life once again.

The ill lose more than some, yes.
But losses can come with gains
Previously unseen, or relegated
To the realm of dreams.

There are lives to touch,
New experiences to have,
Memories to make,
Affections to share.

So—invest fully.
Love deeply.
Sojourn often.
Stay aware of joy.

# DISABLED

We define the disabled in shorthand,
Pity their plight, picture their lives as less than
And move on because we can.

Assigning slighter worth
To experiences not our own
Seems easy enough.

Stereotyping is efficient, we learn,
Inspecting others' lives closely,
Allowing them to change us—less so.

So we become pigeon-holing people,
Shorthand fix virtuosos,
Missing how able the disabled are at

Changing us.

*III*

# THE EXAM ROOM

Much can change in so small a space—
A presumed future,
Life pursuits,
Self-understanding.

I have wondered if some who make diagnoses
Know the power they have
To alter a life's course when
Hardly a word is spoken.

"You have . . . . "

Every exam room
Should have by its doorway
A list of those who, in that space,
Lose the life they knew,

Commemorating all who have to reveal to
Partners and children,
Parents and friends,
Colleagues and neighbors, the

Permanent interrupter,
Game changer,
Life ender.

After all, these are hallowed spaces,
Where one should walk lightly and
Dwell reverently,

Honing compassion,
Offering comfort,
Gesturing hope,

Invoking grace.

# NINE WORDS

Outside the Rector's study,
Books line shelves and
Colorful vestments hang
On a pine rack marred by use.

I shift in the hard chair
As my heart beats quick,
About to speak of imagined life's work
Three days before Easter.

Invited inside, barely 20 years old,
A naked soul bares itself
Before the collared Father,
Who listens but appears unmoved.

He cites the demands of
A week called Holy
Before saying that my youth
Prevents a more developed view.

Trying once more to pierce priestly armor,
Anchored in weeks of rehearsal afar,
His faint smile dismisses,
Quaint words prepare the scars.

"You want to serve?
Become a lawyer and tithe."
With these nine words
A vocation dies.

# The Wise

The wise savor every moment,
Aware that none can ever be kept.

The wise wake with urgency,
Shun the waste of worry,

Cast-off joyless tasks,
Flee from "busyness" chains,

Loath even to say the word.
The clock ticks longer for some,

But always at the same speed.
The wise hone in on its second hand,

Watching its every move,
Hearing each tick.

# THE CUL-DE-SAC

On an afternoon drive,
My daughter and I pull into a cul-de-sac
At the top of a hill and stop in front
Of a house under construction.

Perched on a large lot between
Two immaculately kept properties,
It offers a majestic view of the
Twisting river hundreds of feet below.

Five sunburned men move
Purposefully in this space,
Carefully hammering beams,
Mixing mortar, and moving dirt-filled

Wheelbarrows across smooth,
Imported soil as
The warm sun falls
Slowly into the horizon.

An adolescent girl
About my daughter's age
Sits in a supply truck
Reading a book.

She looks up,
Watches one of the men
Hammering wooden beams,
And smiles.

Stopping to wipe his brow,
He looks up, sees her, and waves.
"Hi Papa!" she says
Before looking back at the book.

I look at my daughter
In the passenger's seat,

Discreetly wiping my eyes.

# INSOMNIA

"I will sleep when I die,"
My quip used to be,
Stamina the prize,
A means to succeed.

"I can outwork anyone,"
Another go-to phrase,
A motivating mantra
Fueling each day.

With a shaking diagnosis,
Harder words came,
Talk of tremors and stiffness,
Every day the same.

At first, my knees wobbled,
But stability followed.
I began to see
Rest helps one feel free.

Is it true, after all?
What we sow, we reap?
With eyes wide open,
I wonder,

Especially at night,
Scanning the darkness,
Wanting to live,
Longing to sleep.

# My Pacer

*(for Mary Beer)*

After illness tripped me,
I became a runner.
You, a runner, too,
Became my pacer.

On long training runs
In hot Texas summers,
Your kindness and
Humor buoying me,

I felt normal,
Less self-conscious,
Confident and hopeful
In a strange new life.

For two marathons you ran beside me,
Adjusting your pace,
Carrying me on your back
When I hit the walls. Lots of them.

Though we may not run
Another marathon together,
Your kindness and compassion,
Your humor and friendship

Will stay with me,
For you changed me.
Now, I carry you
In the longer race I face.

## The Man by the Lake

The man by the lake
Holds a walking stick,
Stands on the bank,
Stares at the waters,

Speaks and chants,
Shakes a fist at the sky,
Squats down near the ground,
Shouts, "I'm not ready to die,"

Opens his arms,
Listens and smiles,
Stands once again,
Says, "I'll see you tomorrow."

# What If?

The anxious live with a persistent *What If?*
What if such and such occurs or if this or that does not?
What if my greatest fears are realized?
Will I ever stop asking, *What if?*

These questions live on the tip of the tongue.
They bubble up from a churning stomach and
Slide past a fast-beating heart,
Silencing, paralyzing, robbing joy.

The day may come
When a new question emerges:
*What if I stop asking What if?*
*And dwell in what is?*

The anxious long for this day,
To live in this way.

# LEVODOPA

I awake early.
Darkness still covers the sky.
I take my morning dose of levodopa.

I begin to run.

My legs feel heavy.
The first miles are hard.
A smooth cadence eludes me.

The levodopa kicks in.

My legs feel lighter.
My pace quickens.
I glide.

The medicine does its work.
I am grateful.
Just as I will be tomorrow?

# Coping

A cinderblock sits on your chest.
Waves of worry crash on your soul.
Sources of dread frequently change, but
Its path stays the same.

The path points to tomorrow,
Toward an openness I once
Deemed more certain,
Controllable and predictable.

Thinking about the future
Brings the future into existence,
Its burdens taxing the present
As if to settle an old debt.

The source of the debt
I do not know.
Nor do I assume I can pay it off
Once and for all.

I know when I feel debt-free:
Watching my younger daughter surf a boat's wake,
Writing poems, hugging my spouse, or
Listening to my older daughter play Chopin on the piano.

Dread abates when
Letting tomorrow not yet exist,
Delighting in what I have today,
Forgetting what I may lose tomorrow.

# DAUGHTERS

*(for Meredith and Holly)*

Who knew that love could so order a life?
When everything else gets in line behind
Ones that fill your heart and then some,
Whom you labor to protect from meanness and strife.

It is getting better for girls and women, we say,
I think this is true, at least on some days,
But misogyny still can rear its ugly head
In what boys and men do, in what goes unsaid.

To the two I love most, I say:
From honoring you I will never rest,
Nor from affirming your power to lead
And show others, including me,

What you know is best.

# In the Care of Plenty

If I am to make peace
With what I have lost,
Thanksgiving must anchor sadness
As commitments moor love.

Seeing abundance before dearth
Quells a longing for what could have been,
Placing me in the care of plenty,
In the rest of enough.